Everyday Wisdom

Volume 1

I0142111

Keidra H. Hobley, PhD

Purpose Publishing

To the first one hundred people who
subscribed to my weekly email. Thank you for
believing I had something to say worth reading.
It is you who encouraged me to consistently
write these daily doses of *Everyday Wisdom*.

CONTENTS

FRESH OIL

When I got to my office this morning, I turned on some music then began to worship and pray. In the middle of the second song, I felt like I had silenced all the distractions but I wasn't being still. I don't mean I wasn't being still because I was walking around as I prayed, but my heart wasn't still and my mind was far from still. My intentions were good but my effectiveness was poor. So, I turned off the music and I sat down. I then began to identify all the things that were racing through my mind and I cast all those cares on God. I could physically feel the weight beginning to lift off of me. I realized I had slowly began to drift back into works – focusing on doing things for the Kingdom without first ensuring I was being who God wanted me to be in the Kingdom. I repented.

A few seconds later, I realized I was sitting in a chair right next to one of those plug-in air fresheners. I leaned down to check it and then I caught myself. "Stay focused, Keidra." I had to remind myself. But there was something within me that just felt like I was supposed to check it. I kneeled down to pull it out and immediately had the thought, "Really, Keidra. Is this what it takes to get you on your knees?" (I know I'm not the only one who has thoughts like this!) I shook off the condemning thought, pulled the plug-in out of the socket and checked it. It was completely empty and dry. It was at that point that I realized it had been three months since I put them in. I then went to the front of the building to check the other one. It too was empty and dry. My first thought was, "I wonder how much longer I could go before I absolutely have to change these out." After thinking about it, it dawned on me that it's probably at this point that the warmers begin to get discolored, unpresentable and you don't want them to be seen. Not wanting that to happen, I went to the next room, got some refills and replaced the empty containers. I then went back, sat in my chair, and attempted to once again be still.

It was only about a minute later that I began to smell something very pleasant. I began to smile as I thought of the sweet Holy Spirit infiltrating my office. Then, it dawned on me... It was the plug-in! I'm not even joking. Just that fast I had forgotten all about it and just that fast it began to permeate the room. Now I smiled for a whole different reason. Just like that, the Holy Spirit showed me something in a way that I can never forget. He showed me the effectiveness of fresh oil! It wasn't like the room smelled bad before, but there was an immediate and noticeable difference once the fresh oil was applied.

We, as believers, have to get to the point where we value and crave fresh oil. We can no longer be satisfied with doing works for the Kingdom when we ourselves are empty and dry. When we allow ourselves to get to this point, others may experience the beauty of our gift but they won't encounter the benefit of our anointing. It's the oil that causes the anointing to flow. If we really want to be potent and make an undeniable impact for the Kingdom, we must be committed to ensuring we have a constant infilling of fresh oil. That's when our lives truly become a sweet aroma before the Lord.

Now, let's see how this applies to you.

What types of things have a tendency to distract you while you're praying?

_____

_____

_____

_____

_____

_____

What are some things you do that help you to be still before the Lord?

_____

_____

_____

_____

_____

_____

What does it usually take to get you on your knees to pray?

_____

_____

_____

_____

_____

_____

Are you an empty container attempting to do good works for the Kingdom? Explain.

_____

_____

_____

_____

_____

_____

Do you attempt to go as long as you can before you refill with fresh oil? If so, why?

_____

_____

_____

_____

_____

_____

Are you hiding because you know you have become a discolored and unpresentable vessel?

_____

_____

_____

_____

_____

_____

What will you begin doing differently today to help ensure you have a continuous infilling of fresh oil?

_____

_____

_____

_____

_____

_____

Study Matthew 25:1-13. What is God saying to you through this passage of scripture?

_____

_____

_____

_____

_____

_____

_____

_____

_____

_____

_____

_____

_____

_____

SEASONS CHANGE

My favorite season is spring. Maybe I like it because it's the season I was born in. Or, maybe it's the fact that it's not too hot and not too cold. Then again, it could be because this is the season where everything that once appeared dead suddenly comes back to life.

Your favorite season may be different from mine. Or, if spring is also your favorite season, it could be your favorite for very different reasons. No matter what your favorite season is, the one thing that's guaranteed is that it will eventually change.

Your least favorite season will come around no matter how long you try to deny it or delay it. It's inevitable.

Just like the natural seasons are guaranteed to change, so it is with the seasons of life. As a single person, it may be the season to focus on your career. As a newly-wed, that season may change to focusing on your marriage. Once your family begins to grow, you may experience an extended season of focusing on raising your children. Once your children are grown and have moved out, you may find yourself in a season of figuring out what season you're in.

We not only experience changes in the seasons of life related to our families, but in every area of life. In our finances we may experience seasons of abundance and seasons of lack. In our emotions we may experience seasons of being up and seasons of being down. We may experience seasons of labor and seasons of rest and the list could go on and on.

We can even experience different seasons as we

walk out God's purpose for our lives. I know for me personally, God has made it clear to me that this is my season to write. While I know there are also other things He has for me to do, this is what He has me doing in this season. I could choose to fight it and attempt to do something else in my own strength or I can choose to embrace it and flow in the grace He has given me.

God's plan for our lives is perfect and He knows every step we need to take to fulfill that plan. Not only is His plan perfect, so is His timing. There are no shortcuts to fulfilling the perfect will of God in our lives. What we have to realize is the fact that trying to do the right thing in the wrong season can be just as disastrous as doing the wrong thing.

We have to recognize and acknowledge what season we're in or we won't be prepared for it. Can you imagine wearing shorts and a tank top in ten degree weather? Or how about a wool coat, hat and gloves when it's one hundred and ten degrees outside? The odds of you surviving a season are drastically decreased when you aren't prepared for it. And if you don't survive it, you certainly won't reap the benefits of it.

Some seasons we enjoy more than others but that doesn't mean we have to waste time in our favorite seasons dreading the day when our least favorite season will arrive. How many times has autumn rolled around and we realize we never went to the beach, we didn't make it a point to wear our favorite sundress, we didn't spend as much time as we wanted to with our children or grandchildren while they were out of school, and we failed to plant that garden yet another year. Many times we miss out on the benefits of the season we're in because we're always thinking about the season to come.

Every season has different characteristics but each one of them has purpose. You may not like the cold of winter, but I'm sure you can appreciate the winter frost helping to control an over-infestation of insects. Everybody looks forward to harvest season but how many of us actually get excited about the season to sow? The Bible says in Ecclesiastes 3:1-8,

> For everything there is a season,
> a time for every activity under heaven.
> [2] A time to be born and a time to die.
> A time to plant and a time to harvest.
> [3] A time to kill and a time to heal.
> A time to tear down and a time to build up.
> [4] A time to cry and a time to laugh.
> A time to grieve and a time to dance.
> [5] A time to scatter stones and a time to gather stones.
> A time to embrace and a time to turn away.
> [6] A time to search and a time to quit searching.
> A time to keep and a time to throw away.
> [7] A time to tear and a time to mend.
> A time to be quiet and a time to speak.
> [8] A time to love and a time to hate.
> A time for war and a time for peace.

You may be in a season right now that you aren't particularly enjoying. Maybe you're in a season of waiting, or in a season of loss, or possibly in some season you never thought you'd ever find yourself in. No matter what season you're in, just know that

God is right there with you in the midst of that season. He promised to never leave you or forsake you. He is perfectly capable of helping you and guiding you through this season. Just remember, how you choose to go through this season just might determine the next season you get to experience.

Now, let's see how this applies to you.

What is your favorite season? Is it spring, summer, fall or winter? What makes it your favorite?

_____

_____

_____

_____

_____

_____

_____

What is your least favorite season? What makes it your least favorite?

_____

_____

_____

_____

_____

_____

What season of life are you currently in? How would you describe this season?

_____

_____

_____

_____

_____

_____

_____

What has God instructed you to do in this season?

_____

_____

_____

_____

_____

_____

Are you doing what God has instructed you to do in this season? If so, explain. If not, why not?

_____

_____

_____

_____

_____

_____

_____

What shortcuts have you attempted to take to fulfill God's will for your life? What was the outcome?

_____

_____

_____

_____

_____

_____

Looking back, have you ever tried to do the right thing in the wrong season? If so, what did you learn from that experience?

_____

_____

_____

_____

_____

Keidra H. Hobley, PhD

Study Ecclesiastes 3:1-8. What is God saying to you through this passage of scripture?

_____

_____

_____

_____

_____

_____

_____

_____

_____

_____

_____

_____

_____

_____

PICTURE YOURSELF

I can recall one morning when I woke up and it dawned on me that my driver's license was about to expire the next week. As I looked at my calendar, I realized it was going to be best for me to go in and renew it that day. Initially, I got frustrated with myself because two months prior I had received a renewal form in the mail that would have allowed me to expedite the process by renewing my license either online or through the mail rather than waiting in the dreaded line at the driver's license bureau. But, the more I thought about it, I realized I wouldn't have renewed it online or through the mail anyway because that would've meant I'd have to live with the same picture on my driver's license for another four years. (Not that my picture was bad or anything. I just wanted a new one.) So with that in mind, I began to do what just about any woman would do... I started looking for the perfect driver's license photo outfit!

It needed to be something not too dressy and not too casual. It needed to be not too plain yet not too flashy. It needed to be not too colorful but not too dull. It needed to have some level of interest around the neckline yet not cover my neck completely. With all these different criteria to meet, finding the right driver's license outfit seemed nearly impossible. There was nothing in my overstuffed closet that I felt met all of these criteria. For over an hour, I searched and I searched and I searched. I tried on this outfit and I tried on that outfit. I tried on this accessory and that accessory. I envisioned what I would look like in certain outfits when I was fully made up and envisioned how my picture would turn out on my driver's license. Finally, I made a decision and decided to end my search. But even then, I still got the sense that my search wasn't really over. Something in me knew I would probably need to invest just a little more time in continuing my search so that my vision could be fulfilled.

Why is it that so many of us are willing to invest so much of our time searching for the things necessary to bring our vision to pass yet so few of us are willing to invest the time that it takes to search for the right pieces to our life's puzzle that would manifest the vision that God has for us. Too often we don't envision ourselves as God sees us and therefore we have no idea when we need to keep searching. We have no idea that something is missing. We have no idea that we don't look the way we're supposed to look. Even sadder, too often we get satisfied with the good we had in our lives years ago and we don't even attempt to envision anything better. We just continue to coast through our lives holding on to our past victories and all the good that we've previously accomplished – all while failing to see that God has new victories and even greater things that He desires for us to accomplish.

When I looked at my old driver's license photo, I was reminded of everything I had to go through four years ago to get that license. If I had kept that same photo, eight years later I would have still been reflecting on those same old victories. I'm glad I took the time that was necessary to envision something new and something even better. I'm grateful I took the time to search for all the right pieces that were required for the vision to be manifested. Taking the extra time to go in to take a new picture rather than trying to expedite the process, has encouraged me to have new vision so I can experience new victories. Not only that, but I have a visual reminder of how far I've come. I'm encouraged to continue to have fresh vision for my future. It's a reminder to not be satisfied with good and to continuously strive for great. As I continue to grow, I'll recognize that what was great in my past may only be good in my present. This means I must continuously strive for new levels of greatness in my future.

Even if my driver's license photo hadn't turned out how I wanted it to, I could have still walked away from that experience knowing the time I invested in the process was not in vain because the lessons that I learned from it will impact me for the rest of my life. Vision must remain fresh. Who wants to invest a lot of time working towards a stale vision? We need to envision the picture of ourselves four years from now being even better than the picture of ourselves today. We need to remember that God has a vision for us and we have to be willing to invest the time necessary to bring His vision for our lives to pass.

Now, let's see how this applies to you.

Describe how you see yourself.

_____

_____

_____

_____

_____

_____

_____

Do you see yourself the way God sees you? If not, how is what you see different than what He sees?

_____

_____

_____

_____

_____

_____

_____

What is God's vision for your life?

_____

_____

_____

_____

_____

_____

How much time do you invest in bringing God's vision for your life to pass? What types of things do you do in that time?

_____

_____

_____

_____

_____

_____

What past victories do you continue to reflect on that keep you satisfied with what you accomplished in the past rather than encouraging you to conquer even more in the future?

_____

_____

_____

_____

_____

In what areas of your life have you settled for good rather than pursuing great?

_____

_____

_____

_____

_____

_____

_____

What are some of the things that were great for you in your past but would not be good for you in your future?

_____

_____

_____

_____

_____

_____

Study Jeremiah 29:11. What is God saying to you through this passage of scripture?

_____

_____

_____

_____

_____

_____

PREPARE TO FLOW

One day last week I was in my closet trying to decide what I was going to wear that day. I finally settled on some white linen pants and a chartreuse top. I took both pieces to the ironing board to prepare them to be worn. I ironed the top with ease but the pants gave me some resistance. They were a bit more of a challenge. I had to crank my iron up on the highest heat setting, spray my pants with water, and apply extra pressure for the wrinkles to be released so the pants could flow like they were designed to flow.

After I got showered and dressed, I gave myself one last look over in the full-length mirror before I headed out the door. I couldn't help but think to myself, "How could such a beautiful, lightweight material that flows like this require so much heat and pressure?" As I pondered the question, it dawned on me that it's no coincidence that linen is the highest heat setting on the iron. In the days of the old testament, God instructed the priests to wear linen. Under the new covenant, Revelation 5:10 tells us that God has made us to be priests to serve Him and to reign on the earth.

In order for us to flow in the beauty of the gifts God has given us and the call He has placed on our lives, we have to go through a preparation process. Don't be caught off guard when the heat is intensified in your life. Know that it's designed to help eliminate every wrinkle that is preventing you from flowing like you were created to flow. Allow yourself to be saturated by the living water of the Holy Spirit so that the heat that's applied to your life can do its work more effectively. Know that the extra pressure that's being applied by your circumstances is simply a reflection of what you're made of and what's necessary to prepare you to flow in your Kingdom assignment.

Often times we see other people flowing with the Holy Spirit in a way that almost seems effortless. We want to be able to do what they're doing but we have no idea what they had to go through to get there. We don't want to go through the trouble of continuously casting our care on the Lord and leaving them there so we can be lightweight, carefree, and flow with such beauty and grace. Too often we don't want to. endure the heat or the pressures of life, but these are the very things that are going to cause us to draw close to God so we can be saturated in His presence. It's when we endure these light afflictions of being tested by the heat and pressures of life that we can be presented to the Father without stain or wrinkle as a living sacrifice. It's at this point that we're willing to die to self so we can live for Him. It is only then that we are prepared to flow with the precious Holy

Spirit like we were created to flow.

Now, let's see how this applies to you.

Are you flowing in the gifts and calling God has given you? If so, how? If not, what's preventing you from doing so?

_____

_____

_____

_____

_____

_____

_____

_____

_____

_____

_____

In what ways do you compare yourself to others that prevents you from flowing the way God created you to flow?

_____

_____

_____

_____

_____

_____

What challenges have you been faced with that attempt to hinder your flow?

_____

_____

_____

_____

_____

_____

What heat and pressure has been applied to your life that you have resisted?

_____

_____

_____

_____

_____

_____

What wrinkles do you have that still need to be ironed out before you can fully flow in your Kingdom assignment?

_____

_____

_____

_____

_____

_____

_____

What cares do you need to cast on the Lord so you're not weighed down and unable to flow?

_____

_____

_____

_____

_____

_____

_____

In what ways do you still need to die to self?

_____

_____

_____

_____

_____

_____

Study Ephesians 5:26-27. What is God saying to you through this passage of scripture?

_____

_____

_____

_____

_____

_____

_____

_____

_____

_____

_____

_____

_____

_____

CLEAN HOUSE

Yesterday I got to have one of those rare days that I call *PJ Day*. I got to stay home all day and didn't even bother to take my pajamas off. I used the time to do something that was well overdue – clean. I put in a full day's work plus overtime. At the beginning of the day, those closest to me made comments like, "What do you even need to clean?" As it got later and later in the day, I started getting comments like, "You're still cleaning?"

Just from looking at the surface, they couldn't understand why I needed to invest so much time into cleaning something that already looked spotless. From what they could see, every time they came over, everything appeared to always be in order. But what I was cleaning yesterday, were those places I don't invite others into. I spent the bulk of my time cleaning out the places that I intentionally keep behind closed doors. And not just behind one closed door but behind multiple closed doors.

I always keep the door to my bedroom closed. It seems to be the only place I get to have to myself. Once you step inside my room, you're greeted by another closed door that leads into my bathroom. Once you make your way pass that door, you're then met by two additional closed doors, which lead to my closets. It's here, multiple closed-doors deep, where the bulk of the cleanup needed to take place.

Sweaters that were once nice and neatly folded on the top shelf of the closet were never replaced after they avalanched as a result of me attempting to pull one out the middle of the stack. Dozens of shoes, that for some reason never seem to walk themselves back to the shoe rack, lay there helplessly enduring the weight of the mountain of sweaters that fell on top of them. Purses were getting all bent out of shape as they are empty, unused and unreturned to their rightful place. Having more clothes than hangers, there are whole wardrobes worth of old clothes that need to go out to make room for the new ones that have come in. It's these unseen, not so obvious areas that required such an investment of my time and attention.

The condition of many of our lives are much like the condition of my closets. We attempt to cram so much into each day that it's inevitable at some point our lives will become overcrowded, overwhelming, and in need of a good cleaning. From the surface we may look like we have it all together, but if we were to allow someone to look behind the areas of our lives that we've kept off limits, they would quickly see how much of a mess our lives really are.

We often spend so much time making sure our

outward appearance is presentable that we neglect to invest the time needed to make sure our inward man is equally as clean. We've made it such a habit of closing the door to our inward disarray, that we're in denial about how out of control it has become. All the areas of our lives that were once nice and neat and in their proper place have snowballed to the point that not only us, but everyone close to us, are being crushed by the weight of our chaos as we get bent out of shape by the minutest of things. Our schedules are packed but we somehow still feel empty, unused and not in our rightful place. Our lives are so overcrowded from the things of our past that we don't have the capacity to embrace the new things that God has in store for us.

No longer can we be accepting of such living conditions. It's time to clean house! We need to stop settling for just being presentable on the outside and start ensuring we're also healthy and whole on the inside. Many of us not only need to schedule a PJ Day to get our physical house in order, but we also need to set aside the necessary time to get our spiritual and emotional houses in order as well.

Now, let's see how this applies to you.

Do you appear to have it all together on the outside but you're actually dying on the inside? Explain.

_____

_____

_____

_____

_____

_____

_____

_____

_____

_____

What unclean areas of your life do you intentionally keep behind closed doors?

_____

_____

_____

_____

_____

_____

Who do you allow to see behind the closed doors of your life? If no one, why is this the case?

_____

_____

_____

_____

_____

_____

What help do you need to ask for in order to clean out the hidden parts of your life so you can live completely free?

_____

_____

_____

_____

_____

_____

_____

Who can you ask to help you in each of these areas?

_____

_____

_____

_____

_____

_____

If someone close to you invited you to take a peek behind their closed doors, how would you respond? What would you do?

_____

_____

_____

_____

_____

_____

What areas of your life are all bent out of shape because you have not done what you need to do?

_____

_____

_____

_____

_____

_____

Who in your life is being crushed by the weight of your chaos? What impact is it having on them?

_____

_____

_____

_____

_____

_____

What things have you attempted to cram into your already overcrowded life that has left you overwhelmed?

_____

_____

_____

_____

_____

What old things do you need to get rid of so you have room to receive the new things God wants to give to you?

_____

_____

_____

_____

_____

Study Psalm 51:1-10. What is God saying to you through this passage of scripture?

_____

_____

_____

_____

_____

_____

EVERY NEED MET

A little earlier today I was having a great conversation with a friend. We had been on the phone for a good little while and I knew my battery was getting low. When I got the 20% warning, I checked my purse for my charger and it wasn't there. That's when I realized I had left it at home. (I can hear your gasps as I type this!)

You would think I'd have another charger in my desk drawer or in my car or somewhere, but I knew I didn't because my main charger had started becoming so unreliable that I had started using my old backup charger as my primary. So, everyday for the last couple of weeks, I've had to remember to put it back in my purse if I had taken it out to charge my phone at home. And the one day I failed to do that, it happened to be on the day I was catching up with a friend and running low on power.

Well, the conversation was too good to end, so I did what any other girl would do... I just kept on talking. Before you know it, I heard the chime of the 10% warning ringing in my ear. "Oh, no!" In that moment, reality started to set in. Not just because my phone was about to die soon, but because I remembered I was expecting an important phone call within the hour!

It was at that point that I began searching every desk in the building... wishing, hoping, praying that somebody at some point had left a charger on their desk that I could use. But to no avail, I found nothing. I went back, sat at my desk and continued my conversation until the inevitable happened... my phone died. As soon as it did I jumped up, closed the blinds, turned off the lights, grabbed by laptop and my purse and headed out the door. I needed to get home to charge my phone before that call came through.

I was in my car, getting ready to start it when the Holy Spirit said, "Check your bag in the trunk." I had thought about checking my bag when I was at 20% but I had convinced myself that I had left it at home also since I was trying to travel light. This time, I didn't ignore the prompting. I popped my trunk, got out, and right there was my bag. Look at God! I immediately unzipped it, went straight to the inside pocket and grabbed the brand new charger I had won at an arcade I took my children to last summer! I grabbed my purse out of the car, went back inside, was able to finish my work and take the call at the designated time. The very thing I needed was available to me the whole time. If only I had listened to that still, small voice that tried to tell me where to go to get what I needed before I was completely drained, I could have saved myself some time and stress and I could have finished my conversation with my friend.

There are so many different directions I could take this story, but the one thing I think we need to focus in on is the fact that there are so many things we think we're missing when in actuality God has already provided them for us. Why was my bag still in the trunk of my car and more importantly why was I playing arcade games at a waterpark in Texas a year ago? Why had I never used that charger before today? Could it be because God knew the prize I would choose would be that charger and that I would stick it in my bag that would be left in my trunk on the very day I needed it to be there? God is faithful! This may seem like an oversimplified example of God's provision, but I've learned to be grateful for the smallest of things so that I'm prepared to value the greatest of things. If God is faithful enough to orchestrate everything that was necessary to get me a charger for my phone so I could receive a phone call, how much more do you think He's willing to do to ensure you have what you need to fulfill what He's called you to do?

Now, let's see how this applies to you.

What is it that you need but don't think you have?

_____

_____

_____

_____

_____

Have you prayed and asked God for it but haven't taken the necessary steps to get it? If so, what steps do you need to take?

_____

_____

_____

_____

_____

Is there anything you need and may already have but don't realize it because it's not in a convenient, obvious, or usual place?

_____

_____

_____

_____

_____

Has the Holy Spirit already told you where you need to go or what you need to do to get what you need but you've rationalized why it won't work?

_____

_____

_____

_____

_____

_____

Have you ever allowed something in your life to die unnecessarily when it was within your ability to keep it alive?

_____

_____

_____

_____

_____

What small things in your life do you need to start being grateful for?

_____

_____

_____

_____

_____

_____

Study Philippians 4:19. What is God saying to you through this passage of scripture?

_____

_____

_____

_____

_____

_____

_____

_____

_____

_____

_____

_____

_____

_____

_____

_____

PREPARATION

This morning I was awakened bright and early. This gave me a chance to spend plenty of time in prayer as well as time to get a nice long walk in. I came back home, showered, got dressed and was so excited I was walking out the door at a really good time. Before I could close the door behind me, it dawned on me I hadn't eaten anything. So, I went ahead and put my things in my car and went back in to get me something to eat.

When I opened the refrigerator, there staring at me was a container of Greek yogurt. "Perfect!" I thought to myself. I can get a couple scoops of that and top it with some fresh blueberries and get back out the door. As I was about to pull everything out, the thought hit me, "I'm probably going to need something with a little more substance than this." Then I was reminded I had just bought a huge container of oatmeal a couple days before. "Yes! I'll make me some oatmeal."

As I pulled out what I needed to make the oatmeal, I was reminded that I bought the biggest container they had because I said I was going to start eating oatmeal everyday for breakfast. Well, if I'm going to eat it everyday, it doesn't make sense to only make one serving. Right? So, I made a pot full. After it was done, I scooped out some for me to eat right away and I put the rest in a big bowl with a lid. Once I put it in the refrigerator, I said to myself, "You know, I could get out the door much faster each morning if I could just grab something and go." That's when I remembered I had saved all these little containers with screw-on lids that would be the perfect grab-and-go size. So I got all the containers out, pulled the remaining oatmeal out the refrigerator and distributed the oatmeal into the individual containers. After all the oatmeal was divided up, I still had containers left over. So, I decided to make as many yogurt and blueberry parfaits as I could until the yogurt ran out. Thinking I needed to get some protein in, I decided on scrambled eggs. And yes, you guessed it. All the extra eggs went into containers as well.

After I finished everything, I put all the individual containers in the refrigerator, stood back, and smiled. Although I was now leaving the house an hour later than I had originally attempted to, I couldn't help but to think about all the time I was going to save every morning for the next several days. Not only was I going to save a lot of time, but I was going to be able to avoid the temptation to grab a pastry or something else with no nutritional value as I was attempting to get out the door each day. Now that I'm thinking about it, it's also going to save me money. Rather than making the mad dash out the door without eating and stopping to get something quick on the way to my destination, I can save that money and use it to prep next week's meals. The cherry on top is that by saving time, calories and money, it will also result in less stress getting out the door in the mornings and less worry about my hips!

While it's easy for us to see the benefit of us preparing our food in advance, we have a tendency to not want God to take the time to prepare our character in advance. When we walk through seasons of preparation, our character is developed to sustain us as we walk out our calling. Even though these seasons of preparation may feel like they're taking an extremely long time, they will ultimately save us a lot of time in the end. When our character is developed, we're less likely to yield to the temptations the enemy throws our way that would get us off track. We pray and ask God for favor, increase and abundance, yet we don't have the character to sustain the provision He's already made available to us. When life throws you a curve ball and you find yourself in the midst of what could be extremely stressful circumstances, your character will play a huge role in how you choose to navigate those situations.

How many times have you prayed for God to use you? Well, the very definition of preparation is the process making something ready for use. We want to be used, but we don't want to be prepped. When our due season comes, we don't want to find ourselves unready, unable or ill-equipped. When God says, "Let's go," we don't want to have to go back in the house to find something to sustain us for the journey. Embrace your season of preparation so that when morning comes, you'll be ready to go.

Now, let's see how this applies to you.

How do you define character?

_____

_____

_____

_____

How would you describe your character?

_____

_____

_____

_____

_____

Ask three other people to describe your character. What did you learn about yourself from their descriptions?

_____

_____

_____

_____

_____

_____

_____

_____

In what ways do you believe your character still needs to be developed to help you successfully do what God is calling you to do?

_____

_____

_____

_____

_____

_____

What are some of the usual temptations the enemy throws at you in an attempt to get you off track? How do you usually respond to them?

_____

_____

_____

_____

_____

_____

As you look back over your life, what are some things you can now see were part of your preparation process?

_____

_____

_____

_____

_____

_____

_____

If God said, "Let's go" today, would you be ready? Why or why not?

_____

_____

_____

_____

_____

Study Matthew 25:10, 2 Timothy 2:21 and Hebrews 11:7. What is God saying to you through these passages of scripture?

_____

_____

_____

_____

_____

_____

_____

_____

_____

_____

_____

_____

_____

_____

IS THAT YOU?

As believers, I think one of our most frequent concerns is hearing from God. Do I hear from Him at all? Why did He stop talking to me? Is that His voice or is that mine? Sometimes we get so consumed with questions about whether we hear Him or not that we end up drowning out His voice with all our own thoughts.

Just today I felt like I heard an instruction from the Father. It was an answer to something I had been praying about. Instead of being excited about Him answering me, my immediate thought was, "Is that You, Lord?" I in no way felt it was the enemy, so what I was really questioning was, "Is that me, Lord?" I'm sure we've all been there where we start to question if we came up with a thought on our own because it's something we wanted to do.

So many of us who genuinely desire to always be in the Father's will can face these types of situations from time to time, and many times more often than we'd like. The good news is I don't do this nearly as much as I used to and even today the thought only lingered for a few seconds. It seems as if as soon as I let the negative thought go, a new thought came. It was a thought I'd never had before. Let me explain.

God's Word tells us His ways are not our ways and His thoughts are not our thoughts. Our natural minds can't even begin to wrap itself around all that God is, does or thinks. However, 1 Corinthians 2:16 does give us hope that we can have the mind of Christ. And just like a good Father would, He gives us plenty of instruction on what we need to do to help get our minds and our thinking more in line with His. Here are just a few examples:

Never stop praying. (1 Thessalonians 5:17)

Study [the Word of God] continually. Meditate on it day and night so you will be sure to obey everything written in it. Only then will you prosper and succeed in all you do. (Joshua 1:8)

Don't copy the behavior and customs of this world, but let God transform you into a new person by changing the way you think. Then you will learn to know God's will for you, which is good and pleasing and perfect. (Romans 12:2)

You will keep in perfect peace all who trust in You, all whose thoughts are fixed on you! (Isaiah 26:3)

We want to live honorably in everything we do. (Hebrews 13:18b)

Honesty guides good people. (Proverbs 11:3a)

But when the Father sends the Advocate as My representative – that is the Holy Spirit – He will teach you everything and will remind you of everything I have told you. (John 14:26)

We have to pray, study God's Word, change the way we think, keep our mind stayed on Him, live honorably so we can have a clear conscious, be honest and walk in integrity, and most importantly trust the Holy Spirit that lives within us. If we are actively and consistently doing these things, at some point we have to trust that our decisions are lining up with God's Word and His will. A step of faith is only really a step of faith when we have to move out on a decision and we're not sure we've heard directly from the Father. If we had every single detail of our lives spelled out for us, we would never be required to take a step of faith. We would simply be robotically responding to commands rather than seeking an intimate relationship with Christ.

Just like you had to accept Christ by faith, you must trust that you hear and know His voice by faith. If you don't feel like you can trust yourself, then trust God's Word. He tells us in John 10 that His sheep know His voice and a stranger they will not follow. Remind yourself of that daily until you believe it. "Thank you, Lord, that I am Your sheep, I know your voice, and a stranger I will not follow." Once your will begins to line up with His will and you refuse to follow the voice of the enemy, you can confidently move forward knowing the steps you are taking will lead you into your destiny.

Now, let's see how this applies to you.

How do you know when you've heard the voice of God?

_____

_____

_____

_____

_____

_____

_____

_____

How do you determine if the voice you're hearing is God's, yours or the enemy's?

_____

_____

_____

_____

_____

_____

_____

What negative thoughts do you need to let go of so new, healthy, godly thoughts can come?

_____

_____

_____

_____

_____

_____

What's the first thing you do when you have a decision to make? Why is that the first thing you do?

_____

_____

_____

_____

_____

_____

What step of faith have you been procrastinating about making and blaming it on God?

_____

_____

_____

_____

_____

On a scale of 1–10, how well are you doing in each of the following areas?

Prayer   1 2 3 4 5 6 7 8 9 10

Studying God's Word   1 2 3 4 5 6 7 8 9 10

Change the way you think 1 2 3 4 5 6 7 8 9 10

Keeping your mind Jesus 1 2 3 4 5 6 7 8 9 10

Living honorably   1 2 3 4 5 6 7 8 9 10

Walking in integrity   1 2 3 4 5 6 7 8 9 10

Trusting the Holy Spirit 1 2 3 4 5 6 7 8 9 10

What do you need to do differently to get some of the lower areas up?

_____

_____

_____

_____

_____

Study 1 Corinthians 2:11-16. What is God saying to you through this passage of scripture?

_____

_____

_____

_____

_____

_____

_____

_____

_____

_____

_____

_____

_____

_____

CHANGE

I'm sure many of you can relate to the type of morning I had this past Sunday. I woke up nice and early, read my morning devotional, prayed and went ahead and got up to get ready for the day. I showered, did my hair and makeup, then threw on a robe to go to the kitchen and pop a quiche in the oven. (One of four I had prepared in advance and put in the freezer weeks ago. Refer back to *Preparation* for more on this topic.) Since I had already picked out what I was going to wear the night before, I was elated when I looked at the clock and saw that I had a full thirty minutes left before it was time to go (and I'm talking thirty minutes before the time I actually wanted to leave which means it was forty-five minutes before I absolutely had to leave).

I was so excited about all the extra time that I wanted to go snuggle up on the sofa with my Bible for a while before I left. As I was making my way, a soft voice of wisdom said, "You better go ahead and get fully dressed before you do that." Thankfully, I listened and obeyed. I grabbed my dress and was about to put it on when I realized it had just a few light wrinkles in one spot. They were barely noticeable but since I had all this extra time, I thought I might as well get it as nice and crisp as possible. I ironed my dress, slipped it on, got it all accessorized and was pleased with the outcome. Only one more assessment and I would be ready to go in record time.

Before leaving for church, I always put every outfit through what I call The Hallelujah Test. "What is The Hallelujah Test?" you may be wondering. Well, I'm so glad you asked. That's when I raise both arms in the air and do a three hundred and sixty degree turn in the full-length mirror so I can be sure I'll be fully free to worship without any fear of providing a peep show to those sitting around me. Well, my sweet little baby doll dress that would have been totally appropriate for just about any other occasion did not pass The Hallelujah Test. It was a little too short for my liking with my arms fully raised. So, I changed.

This time I went for a maxi dress since I knew it would pass The Test. I got out one I had never worn before, pulled off all the tags and put it on. I don't know how this is possible, but even with my highest heels it was way too long! I'm not talking a little too long. I'm talking so long it would be unsafe to try to walk in. Alright... No time to waste. I've got to change. I felt like I was in a real life nursery rhyme. This one's too short. This one's too long. So, surely the next one would be just right!

This time I chose a high-low dress – one that's

high in the front and low in the back. I figured this one would be the best of both worlds. On it goes. Super cute! I went over to the mirror and raised my arms. The low part of the dress passed the test but the high part failed. This nursery rhyme is over. It's time to change.

Before I did, I needed to quickly check on breakfast. Out to the kitchen I went. I added a few extra minutes to the oven and noticed all my extra minutes to get out the door had been subtracted. I quickly made my way back to my room so I could figure out what was next. I pulled out another dress and held it up to me. It was long but not too long. This should be it! I put it on and it came to my ankles all the way around. Yes! But it fits a little too well, if you know what I mean. No! I've got to change again.

I came out of my closet and went to one of my overflow racks (don't judge). There was hanging a cute little dress that I had bought a couple of months ago. It wasn't too short and it wasn't too long. It was a high-low but it passed The Hallelujah Test with flying colors. It was a size larger than I usually wear which made it extra flowy. A quick ironing, a change from gold accessories to silver, a switching out of purses, a selection of the right pair of shoes, and I'm finally ready to go. Instead of being thirty minutes early, I'm now leaving just in the nick of time. I walked out of my room and the first thing my daughter said was, "You changed?" Wondering how she knew that I asked, "How did you know I changed?" She said, "I saw you when you came out earlier to turn the oven back on." "Huh," I thought to myself. I didn't know anyone had even noticed I had changed. I grab a slice of quiche, headed out the door and made it to church right on time.

Never in a million years would I have ever thought I'd have to change that much. If you saw me in any one of the outfits I changed from, you would have thought it was just fine – possibly even really nice. But even though each looked really good, none of them were appropriate for where I was trying to go. In order for you to get to where

God wants you to go, you are going to be required to change. It doesn't necessarily mean the old was bad, but change is the perquisite for experiencing something new. We cannot expect to keep doing the same old things, the same old way, with the same old people in the same old places and at the same time expect to enter into brand new seasons, experience new things, flow in new gifts or reach new levels of freedom. We cannot be afraid of change. Growth requires change. Progress requires change. Obedience requires change. If God is instructing you to make a change in your life, you automatically know it's for your good and His glory.

We won't always know why we need to change. There may be some subtle wrinkles in our lives that need to be ironed out. There may be some things that are fine for us but may cause a distraction for others. Some change may be required in order for us to experience new levels of freedom. There may be things we're trying to walk in that could eventually cause us to stumble and fall. Trust me… It's usually a lot easier to make the necessary change when God initially prompts you than to experience a fall, suffer the consequences, then get back up only to still have to make the same change anyway. The quicker you change, the quicker you'll make it to your destination.

Now, I am in no way suggesting that change is easy. Most of the time it would be much easier to just stay the way you are. Change can be frustrating, time-consuming, and often times will require some extra cleanup as you go. But, when you make the right change, the outcome is usually more beautiful than you ever imagined and the freedom you gain makes the struggle worth every moment. Then, on top of all of that, you never know all the people that are watching you along the way that are encouraged to make a change in their lives because of the change you made in yours.

Now, let's see how this applies to you.

How long does it usually take for you to obey that still, small voice? Why is that?

_____

_____

_____

_____

_____

What changes are God asking you to make in your life?

_____

_____

_____

_____

_____

_____

_____

_____

_____

Why are you so afraid of change?

_____

_____

_____

_____

_____

_____

_____

How many times are you willing to change before you get frustrated and give up? Explain.

_____

_____

_____

_____

_____

_____

What inappropriate things have you allowed simply because you didn't want to change?

_____

_____

_____

_____

_____

_____

What are some of the things other people are missing out on because of the changes you have refused to make?

_____

_____

_____

_____

_____

_____

_____

Study Hebrews 11:8. What is God saying to you through this passage of scripture?

_____

_____

_____

_____

_____

_____

_____

_____

_____

_____

_____

_____

_____

_____

MISSED OPPORTUNITIES

Earlier this week I was driving my children to their respective destinations. As I was approaching a red light, I noticed a car coming out from a side road that was trying to merge into traffic. I stopped at a significant distance from the light to hold the traffic behind me so they could come out. I waited and I waited and they just continued to sit there. Eventually the light turned green and I had to go. As soon as I passed by, I noticed their head was completely down. I have no way of knowing for sure, but it's likely they were on their phone. When I looked back in my rearview mirror, I noticed they

87

started inching up. By then it was too late. Traffic was flowing in front of them non-stop. They would have to wait until everyone passed them by or until the next window of opportunity presented itself.

How many of us have done this in our everyday lives? We allow ourselves to be distracted and end up missing out on so many opportunities. We have someone show us favor and we don't even recognize it because we don't expect it and we certainly aren't looking for it. Often times we receive exactly what we expect and we see only what we're looking for. If we aren't expecting anything supernatural and we aren't looking for anything of eternal value, then by default we're going to miss out on Kingdom opportunities.

So many times we feel like we're stuck when we probably could have been moving forward had we not been oblivious to all the doors of opportunity God has opened to us. The Bible tells us of many opportunities that are available to us but we continuously miss out on so many of them. A lot of these opportunities we miss because we're unaware of them if we're not reading the Word for ourselves and other opportunities are being missed simply because we aren't applying the Word we already know.

Sometimes opportunities are missed because they come disguised as responsibilities. There are certain doors that can only be opened with the key of responsibility. The Bible is full of these. There are so many things God has promised to us that we will never receive because we refuse to do what He has instructed us to do in order for us to receive them.

It's usually at this point that we get tempted to rely on our own strength. When we get tired of waiting, we sometimes end up attempting to force our way which can leave us feeling overwhelmed, disappointed or hurt. Although we probably still end up making it to our destination at some point, we often times arrive later than we needed to and more frustrated than we had to be.

When opportunity comes knocking at our door, we need to be available to answer it. We need to remove any distractions that would cause us to be looking down when we need to be looking up. Opportunity is just that... opportunity. It only adds value to our lives and others when we take advantage of it.

Now, let's see how this applies to you.

When was the last time you felt like a victim as you watched everyone passing you by?

_____

_____

_____

_____

_____

_____

_____

Looking back, were there any missed opportunities you allowed to go by because you were distracted?

_____

_____

_____

_____

_____

_____

What distractions do you need to remove right now to help prevent you from missing the next opportunity that comes your way?

_____

_____

_____

_____

_____

_____

What opportunities have you allowed to pass you by because you didn't want to fulfill the responsibility that came along with it?

_____

_____

_____

_____

_____

What opportunities have you missed because you didn't obey God's instructions?

_____

_____

_____

_____

_____

_____

_____

What doors have you attempted to open for yourself only to find out it was a door you should have never walked through?

_____

_____

_____

_____

_____

Study Deuteronomy 28:1-14. What is God saying to you through this passage of scripture?

_____

_____

_____

_____

_____

_____

_____

COVERED

I was at a friend's house one day when I noticed an antique settee in the very back corner of the garage underneath a lot of boxes, trash and dog beds. I could tell it had been out there for years! Being a longtime admirer of settees, I went over to it and began to remove all of the things that had it buried. As I got the majority of the trash off of it, I noticed the body of the settee was covered by an old fitted sheet that was filthy, stained and wrinkled. I gently pulled back the sheet, being careful to keep all the trash contained within it. Once I did that, I realized that this settee had been newly reupholstered. My eyes lit up! I could not believe something so valuable had been sitting in the garage being used to hold all these things that were being discarded.

I then noticed there was a dog leash that was caught underneath one of the legs. As I bent down to pull the leash out, I noticed there was a second dog leash underneath the opposite leg in the exact same fashion. It was then that I realized that this settee had been used as a pillar to keep the dogs from roaming too far when they were in the garage. I then said to myself, "I have got to get this settee cleaned up and find a place to put it inside where it belongs."

I took each of the cushions off, picked up all the larger debris, vacuumed out every nook and cranny, discarded the dog leashes, cleaned up all the legs and the trim and began to replace the cushions. When I picked up the first cushion, I noticed it wasn't perfectly square. One of the corners was rounded. I thought to myself, "Well, the upholsterer didn't do a good job on this cushion. It's misshaped." I went ahead and put the cushion in position. I then picked up the second cushion and noticed it was perfectly square. I thought to myself, "Now this one they did a good job on." When I picked up the third cushion and realized it also had a rounded corner, it dawned on me that these cushions were designed this way on purpose. They fit into the rounded corners of the settee perfectly. What I thought was a mistake was actually designed that way on purpose. After I figured that out, I repositioned the cushions so that the rounded corners of the cushions snuggled right into the rounded corners of the settee.

Instantly, in that moment, it hit me. This settee is just like so many of us. Valuable yet discarded. Left to hold other people's trash. Not properly positioned which causes others to believe that we're a mistake. Still holding on to the residual of all the dogs that were once in our lives. Not even realizing that for all these years we have always been covered!

The settee was covered by a fitted sheet that

protected it from feeling the full effect of the external factors that could have easily destroyed it. All the trash and stains that were on the sheet would have been on the settee had the sheet not covered it. We, like the settee, have been covered and protected from what could have destroyed us. Yes, maybe we haven't been fully utilized to our fullest potential for years. Yes, maybe we've been carrying other people's trash for years. Yes, maybe we were reduced to hanging out with the dogs. Yet, God somehow manages to send someone along who recognizes our value. They take the time to help us get cleaned up and help us to get properly positioned so that we can be used for the purpose for which we were created. I'm proud to say that that sweet little settee went from living in the garage to being housed in the room that another friend of mine refers to as *The Jesus Room*. (Talk about going from the pit to the palace!)

So be encouraged, my friend. Just because you may be surrounded by things that have been discarded, doesn't mean that you have been. Just because you may feel buried and burdened down by other people's trash, doesn't mean you're going unnoticed. The qualities about you that others think are wrong, could very well be a part of your Creator's intended design. You may feel like you've lost a lot of years but you have to remember that you have been repositioned, restored, reupholstered and given a new garment which make you new! Your value has not been reduced because you have been covered by The Most High God!

Now, let's see how this applies to you.

What is it that you've been buried under that has caused you to minimize your value?

_____

_____

_____

_____

_____

_____

What things from your past are you still holding on to that are not reflective of your true value?

_____

_____

_____

_____

_____

What are you going to do to remove those things from your life and clean up the residual that they have left behind?

_____

_____

_____

_____

_____

_____

What is something unique to you that is tied to your
purpose that others may think is a mistake?

_____

_____

_____

_____

Looking back, what trash and stains should have
adversely impacted you but didn't because you
were covered?

_____

_____

_____

_____

_____

_____

_____

Who has God sent into your life that recognizes your value? How has God used this person in your life?

_____

_____

_____

_____

_____

In what ways have you been made new and more valuable than ever before?

_____

_____

_____

_____

_____

How often are you purposely looking to find value in other people? Give an example of when you have done that recently.

_____

_____

_____

_____

_____

Study 2 Corinthians 5:17. What is God saying to you through this passage of scripture?

_____

_____

_____

_____

_____

_____

SHOW ME THE POWER

A few years ago I bought a lawn trimmer and a blower. When I was looking at all the different options, my two greatest criteria were that they needed to be lightweight and battery powered. I decided on these criteria not because I'm weak but because if we were going to do yard work as a family, I needed tools my children could handle. I would cut the grass and they would decide which of them would trim, pull weeds or do the blowing.

As they got older, my boys would cut the grass, which gave me the opportunity to use the other tools more often. The more I used them, the more frustrated I began to get with them. The trimmer wasn't producing that nice, clean edge that I like. It seemed as if you had to blow over the same spot multiple times just to get one area cleaned. And by the time you got half of the work done, the battery would run out and it would take several hours to recharge.

Well, this was the year I decided I was going to get something more powerful. Not only something more powerful, but I also wanted something more specific. Yes I wanted a more powerful trimmer, but I also wanted an edger – something that was designed to cut that nice, sharp line I was looking for. For months I looked at several different options at several different stores. I compared prices as well as features. Do I want corded, battery powered or gas powered? A straight arm or curved arm? If I go corded, how long of a cord would I need to make it to the farthest point? If I go with battery-powered, how many more volts do I need above what I already have? If I go with gas, do I get one that has to be mixed with oil or not? Tons of options but none of them seemed right.

One day about two weeks ago, my sister stopped by. At the end of the conversation, she mentioned she was going to the store. I asked her what store she was going to and when she told me I didn't think anything about it. A few minutes later, I just felt like I should go with her. We got to the store, picked up a few things and were heading out the door. As we were walking out, I saw an edger and a trimmer out of my peripheral. Wait a minute! I have to go back and look at this!

I checked out all the details. They both ran on gas, so I didn't have to worry about running out of power prematurely. One had a straight arm and one had a curved arm. They were the most reasonably priced out of everything I had looked at so far with similar features. They were both commercial grade, so I knew they would be powerful. That was it. My decision was made. I'm getting these!

I got them home, read the manual, got them

assembled, went and got a new gas can so I could mix the oil with the gas, and was excited to get back home to try them out. They were much heavier than my old equipment and they took a whole lot more muscle and effort to get them started, but they also had way more power! What would have taken me days to complete with my lightweight tools only took me minutes with my powerful ones. Not only was the quantity of time it took to get things done significantly less, but the quality of the results was significantly better. I was elated! Why hadn't I upgraded sooner?

Sometimes we will rightfully make decisions in life based on what those around us are able to handle. We help them, we teach them, and we get them to the point where they're self-sufficient. Then, over the course of time, we fail to reassess. They have grown up and we're still treating them like babes. We could be so much more productive but we're just doing enough to get by. There is so much more power available to us but we're still settling for what's lightweight and familiar. We see our batteries keep running out prematurely, but we refuse to take the steps necessary to get what we need for sustained power.

Now I will admit, there is a price to pay for increased power. It's going to cost you something and it's going to take some getting used to. The more power you have, the easier it is for you to accidently hurt yourself or others. You have to take more precautionary measures when your power increases. You may not even understand it at first, but your body may even feel differently after operating this level of power and will require time to settle back down.

Many of us have access to more power but won't do what it takes to tap into it. On the other hand, some us want more power but don't know how to handle it. Then, there are those few that have accessed greater levels of power and have gotten proficient at operating in it. If that's you, there are people out there who need you. Reach out to someone else and help them. If we can get to the place where we're more powerful individually, then imagine what we could do once we're united.

Now, let's see how this applies to you.

Has there ever been a time where you operated at a certain level to help someone else learn then just got comfortable there? If so, explain.

_____

_____

_____

_____

In what ways have you been frustrated because you're not producing the type of results you'd like to see?

_____

_____

_____

_____

Why do you choose to settle for less power when greater levels of power are available to you?

_____

_____

_____

_____

_____

_____

What steps do you need to take to tap into the greater levels of power that are available to you?

_____

_____

_____

_____

_____

_____

_____

_____

What greater levels of power do you desire but aren't yet prepared to handle?

_____

_____

_____

_____

_____

_____

What spiritual muscles do you need to build before you're ready to carry the additional weight that comes with additional power?

_____

_____

_____

_____

_____

_____

What lightweight and familiar things do you need to let go of so you can trade them in for something more powerful?

_____

_____

_____

_____

_____

Is there any area of your life where you proficiently operate in power and could help someone else? If so, who will you help and how?

_____

_____

_____

_____

_____

Study Acts 1:8. What is God saying to you through this passage of scripture?

_____

_____

_____

_____

_____

_____

_____

_____

_____

_____

_____

_____

_____

Getting wisdom is the wisest thing you can do!

Proverbs 4:7a

IF YOU WERE BLESSED BY THIS BOOK:

- Encourage your friends, family and church members to get a copy.

- Start a small group and go through the book together.

- Subscribe to our email updates by going to https://www.keidrahobley.com/subscribe

- Attend one of Dr. Hobley's live events.

- Read another book by Dr. Hobley.

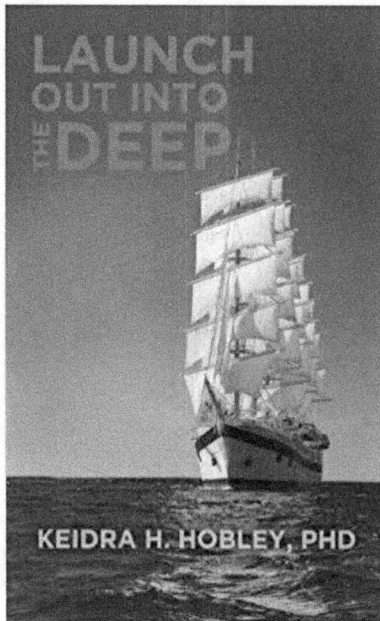

What daily doses of wisdom has God been showing you in your everyday life?

Date: _____

My experience: _____

_____

_____

_____

_____

_____

_____

_____

Wisdom gained: _____

_____

_____

_____

_____

_____

Date: _____

My experience: _____

_____

_____

_____

_____

_____

_____

_____

Wisdom gained: _____

_____

_____

_____

_____

_____

_____

Date: _____

My experience: _____

_____

_____

_____

_____

_____

_____

_____

Wisdom gained: _____

_____

_____

_____

_____

_____